ISABELLA BREGA

Las Vegas

THE BRIGHTEST STAR OF THE DESERT

SMITHMARK

LAS VEGAS

CONTENTS

Text
Isabella Brega

Graphic design
Patrizia Balocco
Alberto Bertolazzi

Editorial coordination
Viviana Valmacco
Alberto Bertolazzi

Translation
Jane Glover

This edition published in 1997 by Smithmark Publishers, a division of U.S. Media Holdings, Inc., 16 East 32nd Street, New York, NY 10016.

SMITHMARK books are available for bulk purchase, for sales promotion and premium use. For details write or call the manager of special sales, SMITHMARK Publishers, 16 East 32nd Street, New York, NY 10016; (212) 532-6600.

Produced by: White Star S.r.l. Via Candido Sassone, 22/24 13100 Vercelli, Italy.

ISBN: 0-76519400-7

Printed in February 1997 by Tien Wah Press, Singapore

1 Known as the capital of gambling, Vegas (as its residents call it) rises like a mirage out of the arid, desolate, Mojave Desert, one of the most inhospitable on earth.

2-3 Las Vegas is the favourite week-end destination for U.S. residents, who are attracted not only by its famous casinos, but by the huge, effervescing hotels, which keep coming up with an astounding stream of ideas to amaze adults and children alike.

4-5 The casino at the Tropicana, one of the many themed hotels in Las Vegas, has every possible kind of entertainment on offer, from slot-machines to video poker, to baccarat.

6-7 The Excalibur Hotel, built like a Medieval manor-house, is one of the most fantastic hotels in Las Vegas which strives continually to stun visitors, with new and futuristic techniques.

8 Las Vegas hotels — here in the photograph is the Imperial Palace seen from Caesar's Palace — are often luxury grade, but cost relatively little in relation to the high standard of the facilities provided.

9 The Luxor Hotel, which cost $390 million, is a 160-metre high reconstruction of a pyramid, the same proportions as the funereal monument at Cheops. The Sphinx is there too and, of course, there is a 60-metre obelisk as well.

10-11 The main attraction of the Treasure Island Hotel, inspired by R. L. Stevenson's book of the same name, is the spectacular sea-battle between pirate ships which takes place without fail four times a day.

12-13 It is not just the gaming which attracts the millions of visitors to Las Vegas every year. The capital of Nevada is also the capital of showtime. The biggest names in music and the most important and newest shows heat up the already boiling-hot nights.

LAS VEGAS, FROM HISTORY TO MYTH

There are times when a bad reputation can do more than any amount of advertising. Las Vegas, state capital of Nevada, is not famous for the startling Mojave Desert which surrounds it, nor for its magnificent geographical location not far from the most striking rock formations of the American West (most especially the Grand Canyon), nor for the nearby Hoover Dam, whose construction on the Colorado river formed the immense Lake Mead, but for the irresistible temptation of its casinos. This city, which for more than three decades has been the indisputable capital of gambling, is a fantasmagorical, bombastic, money pit. A place of 24-hour madness and excess, an uncontested kingdom of casinos, ubiquitous slot-machines — there are one-armed bandits at the airport to provide a noisy welcome for visitors — and Pharaonic hotels which are more like theme parks for the masses of adult children.

Las Vegas (better known as Vegas) arose like a sinful vision glittering with promises in the desert, a place traditionally reserved for temptation. It is a labyrinth of contradictions, a tangle of emotions, a starburst of scenic brainwaves, a vortex of spectacle, colour and sound. It is a shimmering oasis born in the middle of a desert landscape, a gaudy, bizarre, opulent mirage, an apparition in a place whose very name conjures hallucinations. This gambling paradise grew up in the inferno of a desolate plain; one of the world's most lively settlements is located on a baked and sunburnt land, a city with some of the most comfortable rooms and luxurious hotels anywhere vibrates in the immobile air of one of the most inhospitable places on earth. In this obsessive heat, beneath a sky tortured by an implacable sun, in places where more than 250 US nuclear tests have been carried out and where the first UFO sightings were reported, in the land of Extraterrestrial Highway 375, along highways flanked by yellow signs warning of flying saucers and little men with outsize heads, the parameters of normality no longer mean anything and everything is

14 Las Vegas means roulette, dinner, breakfast, shows, slot machines, neon lights, air-conditioning and drinks at any time of the day or night. In contrast with the preconceived idea of the desert as a place where neither life nor joy can exist, Vegas shines like a scintillating oasis rich in sounds, lights, smells, emotions, music and fun.

15 The Stratosphere Tower, one of the most recent constructions which go to make the capital of Nevada something quite unique. Opened in April last year, it has 1500 hotel rooms, seven themed restaurants, 2400 slot machines and 75 gaming tables distributed around its three casinos, shops and, by no means last, three wedding chapels, to get married as close as possible to Paradise. There is a splendid view of the entire city from the top. The 350-metre tower is the highest building west of the Mississippi.

L A S   V E G A S

16-17 The feeling visitors have of being in a movie colossal in MGM's Grand Hotel, the biggest hotel-casino in the world with 5,005 rooms, starts right from the entrance, which is marked by a gigantic reproduction of the lion-symbol of the famous US film studio, Metro-Goldwyn-Mayer. The hotel also boasts ten restaurants, four themed casinos, a swimming pool with real sandy beaches, a concert arena and a theatre.

plausible. No excess seems truly excessive and any kind of madness, especially in the field of architecture, is permitted. As the size and shape of this desert Disneyland, this immense gambling playground, take shape, the line between licit and illicit, moral and immoral, good and evil becomes blurred at the edges, just as the appeals to see vice as a virtue, "sin" as something to boast about, crime as business and gambling as a reason for living, become stronger.
An unreal city takes shape in an unreal landscape.
It is more like a wonderland, with its Camelot, Giza, Imperial Rome, Chinese pagodas, obelisks, circus big-tops, enormous electric guitars, gigantic lion's heads. This is a real city, strong and aggressive, even though it is hard at first to take it seriously, and it is the only kind which could stand up the crushing comparison with the desolation which surrounds it. Every belief, custom, value and prohibition which is valid for the rest of the world comes to a halt at the city gates, besieged by the unreal, atemporal dimension of the desert, a buffer between the known and the unknown, between today's certainty and tomorrow's hope.
It only took a few years for Las Vegas to escape history and enter the realm of mythology. Located on the state's southern border, connected by direct flights to around sixty cities in the United States and by direct charter flights to Mexico, Canada, Germany and the United Kingdom, Las Vegas will be just one hundred years old with the next millennium. Everything started in 1850, with the precious discovery of water by a Spanish Franciscan missionary.
Founded five years later, the city was originally populated like the rest of Nevada by Mormons, but when gold was discovered it rapidly became a magnet for prospectors, soldiers, adventurers, ladies of easy virtue and tough cowboys, even though up until 1903, when the railway was built, it was nothing more than a name along the wagon trail to Los Angeles.
It was the arrival of the railroad navvies which officially marked the birth of a small town, composed for the most part of saloons and brothels.

17 An aerial view of the County Government Center. Las Vegas does not just mean casinos, gigantic hotels and the chance to get married fast at any time of the day and night in the most eccentric of ways. It is also a convention and international conference centre and in November hosts Comdex, the most important information technology fair world-wide.

However, for another couple of decades Las Vegas went on being little more than a supply point on the Salt Lake City-Los Angeles railroad.

In 1931, the construction of the Hoover Dam nearby brought almost 10,000 men looking for jobs on the new building site to what was no more than a dusty village. The town began to grow, especially when the dam was finished and the first tourists began to arrive to view the amazing feat of engineering. The town's first hotel, the Victory, built alongside the railway line, dated from 1910 and right up until the First World War allowed its guests to pay in gold nuggets. 1931, when gambling was legalised in the sober-minded Mormon state of Nevada, marked the beginning of the city's success. The Las Vegas Club was founded that same year (famous for its blackjack with extremely flexible rules) and Harold's Club opened in 1935 with a roulette wheel, poker tables and ten or so slot-machines.

But the quantum leap was not until the Forties, when Cosa Nostra, picking up the scent of success and attracted by the possibility of investing and recycling enormous amounts of cash, made its inevitable appearance. The city of dreams was the result of one man's dream — to create the Monte Carlo of the North American continent amidst cacti and desert sand. Thanks to the determination and intuition of a gangster called Benjamin Siegel, known as Bugsy, who managed to persuade Lucky Luciano and the important New York godfathers to invest right in the middle of the desert, away from the town's centre, the first, ambitious hotel was built along a military road renamed the Strip and the gambling capital of the world began to take shape.

Grandiose and garish, the Fabulous Flamingo luxury hotel, complete with a waterfall, pink hide wallpaper and gold door handles, was designed by George V. Russel (one of the fathers of Los Angeles modernism) and inaugurated by Bugsy at Christmas 1946 to the tune of $6 million, marking the start of what was to be a constant of all the town's hotels: think big.

But even dreams have to be paid for: the Las Vegas of today

18 top Las Vegas Boulevard, better known simply as The Strip, is the great pulsating heart of this gigantic city of entertainment. Eight kilometres long, lined with trees and all kinds of cafés, bars and clubs, it runs right through downtown Las Vegas.

18-19 Circus & Circus is one of the many hotels in Vegas which cater for the needs of the many American families who choose to spend their weekends here. The hotel has a big theme park, the Grand Slam Canyon, and there are trapeze artists, jugglers and tumblers performing in its casinos.

19 top The Palace Station Hotel & Casino, on West Sahara Avenue, has 1030 rooms and suites, four restaurants and a casino with 2000 slot machines.

20-21 The Excalibur Hotel-casino cost $290 million to build in 1990. It is owned by William Bennet who also owns the Luxor Hotel close by, and was designed by Videon Simpson. It looks a lot like mad Ludwig of Bavaria's castles.

22-23 Sam's Town Hotel & Gambling Hall, a modern interpretation of the old West, has one of the town's most unusual casinos: more than 650 rooms in Western style, ten restaurants and fourteen bars.

was born and Bugsy died.

After spending too much and failing to get his creation up and running, he paid for his megalomania with his life. But Bugsy had had the right idea.

One after another, thanks in each case to the Mafia and to Bugsy's successor, Greenbaum, four more hotel-casinos were built on the Strip, Las Vegas Boulevard, which ended up crossing the centre of the town, as well as new roads and even an airport.

In the ten years after Bugsy's death, the same number of new hotels sprang up on the Strip, averaging one a year. Between 1948 and 1955 came the Thunderbird, the sober and respectable Desert Inn (1950, 229 rooms for a cost of $5 million) the glorious Sands (built in 1952 by Wayne McAllister, the first to use the sign as part of the architecture),

24-25 At night, especially on The Strip, Las Vegas is transformed into the city of lights. Hundreds of people intent on having a good time wander from restaurants to casinos and from one night-club to another.

Las Vegas has almost thirty million visitors a year, around 10% of the total US population. Every day almost 200,000 gamblers head for its casinos.

26 The Flamingo Hilton, situated on The Strip's famous Four Corners, is descended from the celebrated Fabulous Flamingo, the luxurious, ostentatious hotel opened in 1946 by the gangster responsible for transforming Las Vegas into the capital of gaming, Benjamin Siegel, better-known as Bugsy. Bugsy's hotel, with its pink leather walls and gold door handles, was designed by George V. Russel.

The first big hotel with a casino inside built on The Strip was the Riviera, in 1955. It was the work, along with other hotels, roads and even the airport itself, of the man who succeeded Bugsy — who had been killed by his Mafia associates — Greenbaum.

the Dune, the Riviera (1955, $10 million, 291 rooms, designed by the France architects of Miami) and the Sahara (1952, $2 million, 203 rooms). They were all built with the intention of being more luxurious, bigger and more glittery than the ones which had gone before. In 1973 the Bally opened its doors, with its 2130 rooms it was the world's biggest hotel.

In a handful of years, thanks to different kinds of deals and tourist packages, the attraction of spectacular shows with international stars — the Desert Inn, for example, was a constant venue for concerts by Dean Martin and The Voice himself, Frank Sinatra — and, last but by no means least, the indispensable air conditioning, the city of everything, which the writer Tom Wolfe defined as "the most American of American cities", took shape in the middle of nothing.

In about forty years the population expanded from 8,000 inhabitants in 1940 to 465,000 in 1980 and there is no sign of this growth slowing down. A survey carried out by the U.S. Census Bureau in the 1990-1994 period alone revealed that with employment standing at 6%, Vegas was the fastest developing American city, with a 26% population increase: from 852,646 to 1,076, 267 inhabitants.

The number of inhabitants is forecast to reach 2 million in ten years. Almost 7,000 people arrive each month, drawn by the low taxes, the prospect of jobs on the casino and hotel construction sites, (although only 10% of the population is employed in areas related to gaming). Pensioners figure prominently amongst these new arrivals.

Vegas, which as several American publications like Places Rated, Your Money or New Choices pointed out, is headed towards becoming one of the main national tourist attractions; thanks to its convenience, climate (with a yearly average of 294 sunny days), personal safety and cost of housing, it is rated the best place to live for elderly people in the United States.

28-29 Fremont Street, covered-in with a metallic structure and lit by more than two million light bulbs, is one of the town's best-known attractions. The pedestrian area was inaugurated in December 1995 at a cost of $70 million and has shops, restaurants and a computer-generated light show with special sound effects: the Fremont Street Experience.

30-31 The computers which operate the Fremont Street Experience can produce almost sixty-six thousand combinations of colour and sound. A 12-metre high neon cowboy welcomes visitors to the Las Vegas Neon Museum which is right to the west of the pedestrian area.

32 Built on the model of Medieval castles, the Hotel Excalibur comprises four blocks of buildings designed like impenetrable manor-house walls, with a drawbridge and even a fire-breathing dragon. The hotel, which looks a lot like the Bavarian fortresses which inspired Snow White's castle in the Walt Disney cartoon, has more than 4000 rooms, six restaurants, two swimming pools, two theatres, shops and several themed restaurants.

33 The Royal Hotel & Casino boasts "only" 236 rooms. The most recent hotel to be inaugurated in Las Vegas was the New York-New York, on 3rd January 1997. It has 2034 rooms and cost $460 million. The hotel is a copy of the Big Apple's skyline and has a casino with a floor area of 7432 square metres.

34 top The unmistakable
fountain at Caesar's Palace
Hotel, without doubt the
town's best-known,
introduces the theme from
which the hotel draws its
inspiration: Imperial Rome.

34-35 Statosphere Towers
overlooks Las Vegas with its
ultramodern mass. In the
Nevada's capital the rush
towards the future is
continuous and, lately,
even chaotic.

35 The statue of Julius Caesar
rises in front of the Caesar's
Palace Hotel, welcoming the
hotel guests coming from all
over the world to visit the
astounding metropoli.

36-37 The Royal Hotel &
Casino also contributes
towards making Las Vegas
one of the cities with the
most hotel rooms in the
world. Many old hotels have
been demolished over the
years to make way for newer
and more futuristic buildings.

38-39 Sam's Town Hotel & Gambling Hall boasts the second biggest casino in Las Vegas, with 2,800 slot machines and 49 gaming tables. The hotel, which is similar to a huge indoor town, as a Western Emporium, a Western Dance Hall and a bowling alley. One of its most popular attractions is the Sunset Stampede, a laser light and water show held every night from 8.30 p.m. to 10.30 p.m.

40-41 A limousine is parked near the Tropicana, a trendy hotel which include a casino, an aquapark, waterfalls and one of the largest indoor-outdoor swimming pools in the world. A special route through the park allows visitors to admire a unique collection of wild birds and animals. Gaming was prohibited in the United States for longer than in other countries. For decades it was only allowed in two states, Nevada and New Jersey.

42-43 The Dive Restaurant is without doubt one of the most original places to go in Vegas. Located on The Strip, the inside is decorated as a submarine and the impression of eating underwater is heightened by the appropriate lights and sounds. Las Vegas offers every kind of cooking, from Italian to French and from Indian to German.

44

44-45 Both photos show two images of the Riviera, one of the many hotels which face The Strip. On 26th November 1996 The Strip witnessed the implosion of the imposing Sands Hotel, built 45 years before by the architect Wayne McAllister, and famous because it was the first of the town's hotels to use its sign as an integral part of its architecture. The 17-floor building will be replaced by a large hotel complex in Venetian style, with 6,000 rooms. Another of The Strip's old hotels, the Hacienda Hotel, which had 11 floors and 1,140 rooms, was destroyed on the last day of 1996, replaced by a Four Seasons hotel.

46-47 Bally's Las Vegas on The Strip is one of the town's biggest and most luxurious hotel complexes. It has 2,814 rooms, six restaurants, a casino and shopping mall and is particularly popular with couple who come to Las Vegas to get married.

48-49 Silver City Casino is one of many places of the kind which make Las Vegas the capital of gaming. Elvis Presley, who performed here in concert many times, paid homage too to the capital of Nevada, in the film "Viva Las Vegas".

50-51 Almost all the Vegas hotels (the Harra's shown in the picture is boat-shaped) have casinos, which are positioned in strategic places and through which it is often necessary to pass in order to gain access to your hotel room. Slot-machines, nicknamed one-armed bandits, are everywhere too: at the airport, near the restrooms or next to lifts. All the hotels aim to attract guests and gamblers with advantageous package tours, offering special deals on journeys and stays.

Silver City

CASINO

DE YOU COME

SINGLE DECK "21"
5¢ VIDEO POKER MACHINES
$3.95 PRIME RIB DINNER
T-BONE STEAK DINNER $4.99

FREE PARK →→

GINSENG B-B-Q
KOREAN & JAPANESE
RESTAURANT

SUSHI

RIVIERA

OFFICIAL
TOURIST CENTER
FREE MAPS

PEPPERMILL
COFFEE SHOP & LO

GIFT SHO

Silver City TWO FREE CHANCES
TO WIN THIS VEHICLE
At Our Welcome Center

52-53 The General Store at Sam's Town, like others of its kind, fulfils the need to keep visitors as far as possible inside the hotels, providing them with the chance to enjoy themselves, gamble, eat and shop.

53 top The Lady Luck Casino & Hotel on 3rd Street, close to the Fremont Street Experience, has 791 and four restaurants. The hotel is reasonably priced and organises all kinds of shows and entertainment.

52 top The Fashion Show Mall, situated on Las Vegas Boulevard, is strategically placed close to the town's principal hotels like the Mirage, the Treasure Island and the Sheraton Desert Inn. It houses more than 140 shops.

52 bottom The futuristic MGM Grand-Bally's monorail provides a direct link between the Metro-Goldwyn-Mayer hotel and the Bally's Las Vegas.

54-55 Planet Hollywood in the Forum Shops at Caesar's Palace is one of the best known places in town. Its main attraction in this restaurant is the film and TV memorabilia, but since last December it has had a rival on The Strip, the All-Star Café. The newcomer is part of a chain owned by champions from the world of sport, like André Agassi or Monica Seles and is decorated with pictures of the biggest stars. It also provides the chance to watch TV transmission of important sporting events sitting in cabins shaped like baseball gloves.

56-57 The main attraction at the Imperial Palace Hotel & Casino, which is furnished in oriental style, is its impressive collection of classic and vintage cars. Located on Las Vegas Boulevard, it has 2,700 rooms and its car exhibits include Adolf Hitler's Mercedes, Al Capone's Cadillac, the Alfa Romeo that Mussolini gave to his mistress Clara Petacci and President Eisenhower's Chrysler limousine.

58 Las Vegas, Queen of the Nightlife, offers visitors the chance to watch all kinds of shows. The hotels compete feverishly to book or produce the best shows. There are also opera, symphonic and ballet productions in Las Vegas's three theatres.

59 The first tourists started to arrive in Las Vegas in 1903, when the area's first railway line, the Los Angeles-Salt lake City, was built and then in 1935, when the huge Hoover Dam was built on Lake Mead to harness the waters of the Colorado river.

60-61 The grandiose Church of Jesus Christ of the Latter-Days Saints recalls the origin of both the State of Nevada and the city of Las Vegas itself, which developed, curiously enough, out of the rigid moral code of the Mormon faith.

62-63 Caesar's Palace, built in far-off 1966 by Melvin Grossman, is still one of the town's most fashionable places. It cost $25 million to build and is a gigantic kitsch interpretation of the Roman Empire: tripods, statues, busts, improbable centurions and a profusion of polyester tunics à la "Quo Vadis".

BETWEEN DREAM AND REALITY

There are no half measures in the United States, not even in gaming, which, like sin, is organised here on a macroscopic scale. Around 200,000 people come to play in Vegas every day, while the annual attendance in the Nevada state capital and Atlantic City is higher than that of all the European casinos put together. Its gaming rooms make an annual profit of $3.5 billion, roughly the same as from total sales of cinema tickets throughout the entire country.

But it is not just the green baize tables which attract the almost 30 million visitors a year (with 1998 estimates standing at 37 million), almost 10% of the population of the United States. Its allure is based on its choreography, on its grandiose hotels with their improbable historical reconstructions, on the characteristically American conviction that in order to be successful everything must be excessive, showy and gaudy: as personified by Zsa Zsa Gabor, Jerry Lee Lewis or Liberace (the brilliant but eccentric, extrovert pianist to whom Las Vegas dedicated, perhaps unsurprisingly, a museum — one for the Guinness Book of Records), as represented by the Vegas hotels-cum-casinos which, huge, self-satisfied and megalomaniac, make this town which has grown out of all sense and proportion, like disorderly dough, into a Barnum's Circus. On the other hand, as the post-modern ideologue Bob Venturi rightly pointed out in his "Learning from Las Vegas" published in 1972, in Las Vegas, where yesterday's fashion and dreams become tomorrow's reality, buildings should not be judged according to the canons of good taste, because each building is a signal.

The families, who today pour into the state capital of Nevada each weekend and who comprise the majority of the tourists, are very different from the visitors billionaire Howard Hughes, owner amongst other things of no less than four casinos, wished for. Hughes said that when he thought of Las Vegas he saw a man in evening dress and a beautiful bejewelled women, getting out of a luxury car and

64-65 Every year the number of gamblers in the only two American gaming centres, Las Vegas and Atlantic City, is a good deal higher than the figures recorded in all the casinos in Europe added together. The gaming establishments in the Nevada state capital make a total annual profit of almost $3,5 billion, almost as much as the sales of cinema tickets in the whole of the United States.

66-67 The photo shows the slot-machines area of the Imperial Palace Casino. The Nevada city, the capital of gambling, of has inspired many films, from "Bugsy" with Warren Beatty, to "Honey, I shrunk the kids", "Indecent proposal" and "Rain Man". The most recent include "Showgirls", "Casino" with Robert De Niro and Sharon Stone and "Leaving Las Vegas" with Elisabeth Shue and Nicholas Cage.

68-69 Gogol maintained that all men with a hand of cards were equal in a card game, which perhaps makes Las Vegas the most liberal and democratic city in the United States. Not only does everyone have the chance to try their luck, but everyone also has access to the relatively cheap luxury of its amazing, fantastical, hotels.

70-71 The photo shows the big hall of Sam's Town Hotel & Gambling Hall, one of the bigger casinos in Las Vegas. Entry into the casinos is generally free, along with the first drink and, unlike similar establishments in Europe, there is no particular dress code.

he expressed the wish that the place should not be allowed to deteriorate into some sort of side-show.

Now Vegas is perhaps very similar to the kind of side-show the eccentric Hughes was thinking of: excessive, colourful, sassy, showy and dominated by a constant atmosphere of being in a Cecil B. DeMille colossal, with an over-the-top script rolling all the time. A town which has definitely lost a bit of its sinful allure, but not its ability to attract.

Even if the cigar-smoking gangsters in their pinstripes and the beckoning sirens in lamé have given way to middle-aged couples with blue-rinsed hair and quiet family groups in Bermudas and baseball caps, this is still an amazing place; the land where hope flowers and wishes catch fire, something that not even the cinema's inexhaustible imagination has ever been able truly to reproduce.

This is where America realises she is sinful, reveals herself and her taste for excess, in a perfect reflection of what one expects her to be: megalomaniac, transgressive, inimitable — the place where everything is possible, the Land of the Great Opportunity. This is the last American boom town, one of the few which can still afford to ignore ecology, thrift and moderation. Everything, from water to power, from food to alcohol, is joyfully consumed.

Surrounded by a monotonous, sterile environment like the desert, it is an explosion of life, an exhilarating concentration of vitality. Vegas means roulette, slot-machines (women's favourites, strategically placed wherever people have to wait, even in washrooms), compulsory itineraries which force hotel visitors to pass through the casinos, all kinds of shows, huge, cheap dinners and breakfasts, available all the time, whatever the time, free drinks to keep clients glued to the tables, polar air-conditioning, no clocks, 24-hour loan agencies, hotels which refuse to transmit CNN for fear that breaking news might distract or upset the players.

Nicholas Pileggi, who designed the sets for the film Casino, says that Vegas is the second-chance city: those who live there are inevitably fugitives from something, whether it is a divorce, a crime, failure at work or in love.

Las Vegas

LAS VEGAS

72-73 Forum Shops at Caesar's Palace is considered one of the town's most famous and best-stocked shopping centers. Set in a reconstruction of a Roman forum, with a host of Pompeiian buildings topped with statues, huge ornate fountains with winged horses and tritons, marble columns and braziers, it has more than seventy prestigious boutiques, with names like Armani, Bulgari, Christian Dior, Versace, Gucci, Louis Vuitton.

It is a paradise without a memory, without time and without a history, hounded by the need to renew itself in continuation and where everything — from the hotels to the international stars who perform there, to the world boxing contests, to the almost 3,000 huge conventions held there each year (with an economic impact on the city of almost $3 billion), to fairs like Comdex, the biggest in the IT sector — is transformed and sold as a gigantic spectacle. The triumph of the superfluous and the frivolous, of ostentation and waste, even though the real protagonist, hidden below all the lights, feathers and sequins, remains the same: the game, the great puppet-master who moves the cogs of this giant with made-up eyes,

covered in 35 million light bulbs.

Life in Las Vegas canters frenetically Downtown and gallops along the Strip, 18 kilometres of fireworks crowned by hotels, casinos and night clubs of all kinds, the crazy heart of this crazy city: a river of lights, neon strips and billboards, which catches fire at sunset.

When the desert cools down and the night heats up, men and women career along the Freemont Street Experience — a covered pedestrian precinct, the recent $70 million-transformation of five Downtown blocks into a computerised spectacle of lights and music — like the balls in a huge pinball machine, bouncing crazily from a restaurant to a

74 Every year on average 100,000 couples decide to pronounce the fatal "I do" at Las Vegas: one every five minutes and twenty seconds. The famous people who have got married here include Elvis Presley, Paul Newman, Bruce Willis and Brigitte Bardot. St. Valentine's Day and New Year's Eve rank high amongst favourite dates.

75 The Little White Chapel, recognisable by the sign outside with the huge heart and the words "Joan Collins and Michael Jordan got married here" is certainly one of the best known of all the 50 Wedding Chapels. For a few ten-dollar bills they will rent out everything you need: from the limo to the ring, the witnesses, clothes and flowers. Even the most unusual requests, such as having the ceremony performed in a hot-air balloon, in a helicopter, on the edge of the Grand Canyon - can generally be met.

76-77 To get married in Las Vegas you need to be 18 years of age and have a marriage licence issued by the local registry office. You need neither have a birth certificate nor undergo any blood tests.

club, from a hotel to a casino, from a bar to a shop. Nothing, no matter how real it looks, is what it seems in Vegas. Within this distorted and altered reality, inside this upside-down world, what is false becomes true and everything is relative. The empire of light triumphs over the shadows of the night and if, in the classical exception, sin is associated with darkness, like a giant Christmas tree Vegas shines out in the darkness of the desert in all its innocence.

The innocence of those who gamble and the innocence of those who swear eternal love, for green baize tables are not the only speciality here. Las Vegas, whose very name spells out the risks of life, has made instant marriage, and of course, swift divorce, a profitable local industry.

Love and money, future promise as well as possible failure, the two engines of the world drive the Vegas machine too, as it bets not just on money, but also on the heart.

Here, where every dream, even the most eccentric, has a chance of coming true, you can celebrate the most serious of commitments in the weirdest of ways. Motor-bike weddings, weddings in hot-air balloons, in an aircraft flying over the city, on the edge of the Grand Canyon, in the presence of an Elvis double.

Many Hollywood stars have married in Las Vegas, including Paul Newman and Richard Gere. Almost 100,000 weddings are carried out here every year, in particular on St. Valentine's Day or New Year's Eve: 275 a day, one every 5 minutes and 20 seconds. All the participants' need is to have reached the age of 18, to be in possession of a passport and 35 dollars, in order to enter one of the Wedding Chapels which, in contrast to the Pharaonic luxury of the hotel-casinos, have a false, sugary simplicity about them and boast names such as The Little Chapel of Flowers, the Little White Chapel or the Little Church of the West. Thirty-five dollars to gamble, amongst huge pink hearts, flowered arches, refrigerated bouquets and Astroturf, on marriage. For those really in a rush, everything, with the exception of the bride or groom, can be hired, at any time and in any style: decorations, witnesses, celebrants, clothes, videos and limos. The honeymoon?

Casinos, casinos and more casinos are not all Vegas has to offer. There are three theatres which host ballet, opera and symphony concerts; in May there is the Helldorado, the huge Western festival with rodeos, parades and beauty contests, which harks back to this frivolous city's crude beginnings; local travel agents offer interesting trips to natural beauty spots close to the city, like Great Basin National Park, Death Valley, Bryce Canyon or Zion National park, cruises on Lake Mead and guided tours into the Mojave desert.For those who are interested, there is no lack of museums, like the Las Vegas Natural History Museum, the Las Vegas Art Museum, the Lied Discovery Children's

Museum which is only open to children, or the Nevada State Museum & Historical Society, dedicated to the region's ancient cultures. Third in importance in the State for number of visitors, around 150,000 every year in a constant stream of coach parties and tourist groups, the Liberace Museum is housed in a Spanish colonial-style building and is entirely dedicated to the famous pianist. In the city of hyperbole, there had to be a homage to the eccentric musician who loved to cover his cars, clothes and pianos (pink where possible) with a shower of sequins and paste jewels and boasted of chinchilla coverlets on his beds.

78-79 The Liberace Museum is housed in a Spanish colonial-style building, entirely dedicated to Wladzin Valentino Liberace (1919-1987), the eccentric pianist who was known for his lamé suits and his thick black Elvis-like hairstyle, as well as his eccentric pianos. He ended his career on the Las Vegas circuit and every year 150,000 visitors come to see the museum, making it the third most popular tourist site in Nevada. The museum's three exhibition pavilions show, amongst other things, a Baldwin grand piano covered in glittering paste stones, as well as a Rolls Royce, an Excalibur and a coral pink VW Beetle Cabriolet. Paste and sequins cover the velvet cloaks Liberace collected and many other objects belonging to the exuberant pianist. The library displays not books, but pieces of Mozer Bohemian crystal. Don't miss a chance to see the bedrooms and Liberace's own mortuary, with its chinchilla-fur bed cover.

80-81 Las Vegas does not only cater for those who love to gamble. The Nevada state capital has several museums, like the Las Vegas Art Museum, the Lied Discovery Children's Museum (reserved for children only) or the Las Vegas Natural History Museum. The latter houses a notable collection of Native-American objects and a series of specimens of the flora and fauna of the Mojave Desert, the arid territory rich in cacti, yuccas, sand and rocks, which surrounds the city. Situated close to some of the most impressive rock formations of the American West, Las Vegas grew up on a spot not far from where the first American nuclear tests were carried out.
It is also where the most shattering UFO sightings have occurred, in fact the city periodically plays host to international conferences and meetings on the subject of the possibility of extra-terrestrial life.

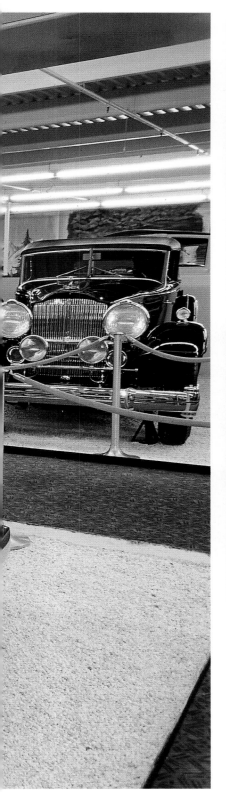

82-83 The car collection belonging to the Imperial Palace Hotel & Casino is a triumph of chromium-plating and stuffed leather seats. Every car reflects the trends and tastes of the era in which it was built. Some of the exhibits are particularly interesting, like the 1906 Ford K Touring, six cylinders, forty bhp, original cost $2,500. There is a 1930 V-16 Cadillac Sport Phaeton, a 1910 Thomas Flyer, famed for its speed and its breathtaking lines and a 1913 Ford T "Pie Wagon". The Imperial Palace auto museum would not be complete without a 1947 Tucker, considered at the time of its launch to be one of the best cars on the road. Unfortunately the company closed down after producing just 51 cars.

84-85 Aquaparks are children's favourites the world over and the world's gambling and entertainment capital could be no exception. This one not only provides an opportunity for fun, it also offers escape from the overpowering grip of the heat which tortures Las Vegas, which is surrounded by the desert.

THE HOTEL FOLLIES OF
LAS VEGAS

They call them the hotel follies of Las Vegas, but what else could one expect in the capital of entertainment and excess. They have been the prime movers in changing the face of Las Vegas and turning it into a tourist attraction for families, harmless pensioners and newlyweds, and in imposing the frenetic rhythm which characterises the architecture in this extraordinary town. Nothing else changes continuously like they do, in line with the same old rule: renewal in order to stay the same as they are, unique and inimitable.

There is only one imperative: stay out in front; only one creed: excess. Forever undergoing extension and rebuilding work, in order to keep ahead of the competition in terms of experimentation and extravagance, there is no doubt that they are the most original product of this original city.

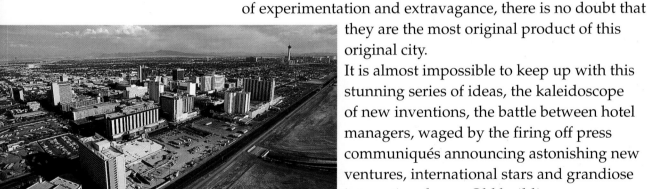

It is almost impossible to keep up with this stunning series of ideas, the kaleidoscope of new inventions, the battle between hotel managers, waged by the firing off press communiqués announcing astonishing new ventures, international stars and grandiose interactive shows. Old buildings are demolished to make way for new ones, projects for the creation of hotels and casinos, even outside the town centre, are constantly being presented.

Gogol used to say that a hand of cards makes all men equal and this gaming capital is without doubt the most liberal and democratic town in the United States. This is where the image of a health-conscious America smashes into smithereens. Tobacco and alcohol taboos are ignored, in fact their national consumption records are proudly exhibited, while everyone has the chance to enjoy the reasonably-priced luxury of its legendary hotels, the only buildings which mean anything in the city. The hotels have no need to charge high prices for the high-level service they offer: the green-baize tables will balance their books for them. Everything has a single aim: to urge people to gamble. Anyone over 21 years of age can enter the casinos that

86 With direct flights linking it to the principal American cities and charter flights to and from Mexico, Canada, the United Kingdom and Germany, Las Vegas has been growing rapidly in popularity since 1931, when the Las Vegas Club, soon to be famous for the extremely elastic rules of its blackjack games, opened its doors. Four years later Harold's Club opened up, with roulette, poker tables and slot machines.

87 The Luxor Hotel employs something like 4,000 people, from croupiers to walk-on extras, from waiters to cooks. Inside its gigantic foyer - one of the biggest ever built, it could comfortably house nine Boeing 747s - designers have recreated a pre-Columbian temple, New York's Times Square and a City of the Future. Guests to the hotel can also admire a reconstruction of an ancient tomb of the Pharaohs.

88-89 The Treasure Island, famous for the working model of an English Navy frigate over 30 metres long, as well as for the 70-minute sea battle between buccaneers and the English Navy which is tirelessly refought four times a day, was built on the ruins of the wonderful old Sands Hotel.

constitute the nerve centre of almost every hotel: there is no need to pay for entry (and often the first drink is free). Even beginners need not worry, the hotels themselves organise free courses for them.

There is one problem only: how to attract the maximum number of customers and ensure that instead of wandering blindly from one club to another or one casino to another, disorientated by billboards, neon signs, lights and adverts, they remain prisoners of the hotels, captured by the thousand and one opportunities these microcosms provide.

Microcosms (the first was the Moulin Rouge Hotel, which opened its doors "long ago" in 1955) which allow guests to sleep, eat, gamble, shop and take in shows and concerts, all beneath the benevolent wing of the munificent and magnificent hotel, the dispenser of pastimes and entertainment, of dreams and happiness. And there is only one way to do this, which is to supply, along with the gaming tables, slot-machines, restaurants, shops and theatres, one folly after another. In this way, Las Vegas loses its diabolical aura, forgets about the gangsters and Cosa Nostra and transforms itself into the Mecca of family entertainment. Technicians and architects work continuously to prepare sites which are more like huge film sets, sets where directors and scene designers wander casually around in an effort to make everything an attraction, providing special effects à la Walt Disney which amaze and entertain old and young alike: fire-breathing dragons, galleons and naval battles, monsters, rapids, treasure islands, tropical jungles, erupting volcanoes. In this context, it ends up being normal to go shopping in a Roman forum at Caesar's Palace, have a drink in the Obelisk Bar in Luxor, eat like King Arthur at the Excalibur, be welcomed by pirates at the Treasure Island and wander around with clowns and trapeze artists at the Circus & Circus or be button-holed by the Wizard of Oz at the MGM. Despite the continual changes, many hotels dating from the historic heyday of Las Vegas, like the Riviera or the Flamingo (which puts up a million-dollar jackpot every year and has the most expensive slot-machine in the world, which can eat

90-91 It is some time now since Las Vegas lost its legendary and at the same time vaguely diabolical reputation as the capital of all vices. It has transformed itself into the most harmless of family wonderlands. It is like a gigantic film set, where technicians, architects, directors and designers are continually involved in producing new, fantastic, showpieces, packed with special effects.

up to half a million dollars a day as it feeds on its $25 tokens) are still up and running. Some, like the celebrated hotel built by Ben Siegel, immortalised in Bugsy with Warren Beatty, impersonate themselves in the many films which the capital of Nevada has inspired: "Honey I shrunk the kids", "Indecent Proposal", "Rain Man", "Showgirls" and, recently, Martin Scorsese's "Casino" with Robert De Niro and Sharon Stone and Mike Figgis's "Leaving Las Vegas", with Elisabeth Shue and Nicholas Cage. Some other buildings have been less fortunate, however, and have been demolished to make way for new, futuristic dreams. But in Las Vegas not even The End can avoid being transformed into a spectacular finale, which is what happened in 1993 when the old Dunes hotel was knocked down to make way for the Treasure Island. The demolition was an excuse for a party and Scorsese used it in the final of Casino. The same thing happened to one of the best known and until not long ago the tallest (106 metres) of the town's hotels, the Landmark, inaugurated in 1969 and knocked down on 7th November 1995 with over 50 kilos of dynamite, before a crowd of thousands, to make room for car parks and conference centres. The great show was filmed by Tim Burton, director of "Batman" and Warner Bros's executive, to use in his film "Mars attacks Earth".

The luxurious, rust-proof Caesar's Palace, built by Melvin Grossman in 1966, is the undisputed king of the town's hotel-casinos. It cost $25 million and is one of the few 30-year old buildings (a huge age by Las Vegas parameters) still to be riding the crest of the wave, the first to pander to the Las Vegas craze for omnipotence and open the way for entertainment hotels. The triumphant world of the Roman Empire revisited in kitsch, reinterpreted in the key of American taste and fantasy: a profusion of fountains, columns, tripods, catacombs, statues and busts, chariots, unlikely-looking centurions with polyester tunics, leggy girls with mini-tunics courtesy of Quo Vadis, laurel wreaths, triclinium-style couches and 1,518 sumptuous rooms. All served in a sauce including two theatres, gaming at the green tables of

92-93 Renowned for having some of the most eccentric hotels in the world, the Vegas contenders fear no comparisons. Despite the passing years, the celebrated Caesar's Palace has lost nothing of its kitsch appeal. It pointed the way for the city's grandiose, fantasmagorical hotels, inaugurating the fertile vein of the creative reconstruction of history so beloved of the city's architects. Nevada's capital city does not know what the word recession means. Even though only 10%

of its inhabitants are connected to the gaming industry, every month around 5-7,000 people move into the Vegas metropolitan area, making it one of the fastest growing cities in America, attracted by the construction of new hotels, restaurants and clubs.

94-95 The luxurious Caesar's Palace hosts conventions and exhibitions of all kinds every year. The hotel is also famous for the shows produced in its own two theatres.

96-97 The Forum Shops gallery inside Caesar's Palace, with a big central fountain decorated with winged horses and tritons, is one of the best-stocked in town. Nicholas Pileggi, set designer on the Martin Scorsese film "Casino", maintains that Las Vegas is the second-chance city: people who live here have inevitably escaped from something, a divorce, a crime, a failure at work or in their love life. Only Las Vegas can guarantee rebirth.

LAS VEGAS

98-99 Thanks to its many hotels like the Luxor, Caesar's Palace, the Imperial Palace or the Excalibur (shown here), today Las Vegas boasted just under 100,000 hotel rooms. Amongst the recently inaugurated hotels are: the Stratosphere, the Monte Carlo, the New York-New York and the Orleans.

100-101 The Luxor Hotel, which is owned by Circus Circus Enterprise, has a power laser ray which can be seen by aeroplanes flying over Los Angeles, 400 kilometres away.

102-103 The spectacle of the eruption of the 16-metre high, three-storey cement volcano which stands in front of the Mirage Hotel can be seen every thirty minutes and is one which no Las Vegas tourist wants to miss.

its three casinos, dinners in the nine restaurants named after the ancient gods, predictions by medieval fortune-tellers, appearances by Caesar in person and shopping in the Forum Shops, the best-known and best-stocked in town, set amongst fluffy clouds and blue skies, a twenty-metre-long chandelier (with 16,000 bulbs and 100,000 pieces of glass), fountains, statues of winged horses, braziers and Pompeiian buildings surmounted by statues. It is a short step from the Imperial Caesar's Palace to the Pharaonic Luxor. The triumphal Roman colonnades give way to a concentrate of ancient Egypt: a gigantic glass pyramid, 160 metres high (30 floors) reproduces the funeral monument of Cheops, flanked by a 60-metre reproduction of the Luxor obelisk, watched over by a replica of the Sphinx at Giza, miraculously completed by the nose destroyed by the Turkish bombardments, and eight navigable miles of the river Nile. It is not just the style which is Pharaonic, the size is too: built in 1994 at a cost of $390 million, it has the most powerful laser beam in the world — 315,000 Watts. It employs 4,000 croupiers, waiters and extras and has 2,526 rooms, seven theme restaurants, 25,000 slot-machines and 500 gaming tables. Its immense foyer, the largest ever built, could fit no less than nine Jumbo jets inside it and houses the fantasy reconstructions of a pre-Columbian temple, New York's Times Square and a futuristic city: the main square, through which every route leads, includes the casino, of course, the apartment blocks house the rooms, the patio with swimming pool corresponds to the park, the bars are the cinemas and the showrooms are the theatres. Time travels, 1600 square metres of videogames, interactive adventures, futuristic shows, complete what this hotel has on offer — as well as a reconstruction-museum of the tomb of the Pharaoh Tutankhamun. Towers, turrets and red and blue pinnacles: the $290-million American version of Camelot at the hotel-casino Excalibur was built in 1990 by William Bennet (owner and creator of the neighbouring Luxor, to which it is connected by an elevated walkway) to a design by Videon Simpson and recalls the Bavarian castles of the mad king Ludwig which inspired the castle in Walt

Disney's Snow White: four blocks of buildings stand guard like impenetrable walls over a fortress complete with drawbridge.

The kingdom is composed of 4,032 rooms, two swimming pools, two theatres, dozens of shops, a fire-breathing dragon, six restaurants and several different eateries with emblematic and rather irreverent names like Sherwood Forest Cafe, Robin Hood's Snack Bar and even Hansel & Gretel's Snack Bar (as in the case of the fortune-tellers at the Caesar's Palace, coherence is not the forte of Las Vegas hotels).

You can eat here admiring an imaginary English landscape, eat in the medieval manner with your hands, watch tournaments or trained white horses perform or even get married in the Canterbury Cathedral annexe, with clothes and a nuptial banquet, all in matching style.

But the biggest of the hotel-casinos, not just in the city of Las Vegas but in the whole world, is the MGM Grand Hotel: 5,005 rooms — it would take 13 years and 8 months to sleep in them all.

On top of which there are ten restaurants, four themed casinos (whose total floor area is the equivalent of four football pitches) a swimming pool with real sand, a fitness centre, tennis courts, parking for 6000 cars, an arena for concerts and boxing matches, three theatres, a 30-acre theme park, an 800-ton fountain, 93 lifts, 8000 employees (including 500 chefs), a heating system which uses as much power as a town of almost 6000 inhabitants.

The whole thing is preceded by the enormous MGM gilded lion's head (which contains the reconstruction of the land of Oz from the Wizard of Oz) which is connected to Bally's Las Vegas by a futuristic monorail system.

Inaugurated in December 1993 at the cost of billions of dollars, extended in mid-1995, restructured in 1996, the MGM develops themes from the golden age of cinema and almost any stroll through its enormous spaces, where visitors will meet film characters, becomes a gigantic quiz about the famous studio's films and cartoons.

104-105 The giant lion's head, 27 metres high, which is actually the entrance to the equally gigantic MGM Grand Hotel, houses a reconstruction of the town in the film studio's famous film, "The Wizard of Oz". The entire hotel complex is decorated on the film's theme. Guests might run across walk-on actors taking the parts of the film's main characters: Dorothy, Toto, Tin Man, Lion, Scarecrow and the Wicked Witch of the West.

106-107 The MGM Grand Adventures Theme Park is the giant fun park located inside the hotel of the same name. New Orleans Street, French Street, Old England Street, New York Street, Salem Waterfront or Asian Village - these are just some of the streets and squares which have been reconstructed in the park in the corresponding architectural style, and visitors walking around them will meet characters from some of MGM's most famous films and cartoons, like Popeye, Betty Boop or Olive Oil.

108-109 In addition to the themed streets and the extras presenting characters from the film studio's greatest hits, the Grand Adventures Theme Park also has restaurants, fast food joints, two theatres, a wedding chapel and the Grand Canyon Rapids and Over the Edge rides.

110-111 The numbers involved in MGM's Grand Hotel are impressive: 5,005 rooms, ten restaurants, four themed casinos, a swimming pool with a real sandy beach, a fitness centre, tennis courts, an arena for concerts and boxing matches, three theatres, a theme park, an 800-ton fountain, 93 elevators, 8,000 employees (including 500 cooks) a heating installation which uses as much power as a village of almost 6,000 inhabitants.

112-113 The Monte Carlo, inaugurated in June 1996 at a cost of $375 million, is one of the most recent Las Vegas acquisitions. The hotel, which is built in the architectural style of the Principality of Monaco, has more than 3,000 rooms.

Circus & Circus, on the other hand, has a huge imitation circus big-top. It has 2800 rooms, a square kilometre of family-style hotel-casino, where the green gaming tables are flanked by the acrobatics of trapeze artists and tight-tope walkers who perform, together with acrobats and dancers, to the sound of a band. There is an amusement park too, of course, called the Grand Slam Canyon, with a big dipper whose peaks are modelled on the mountains of the Grand Canyon itself.

The attraction at the Treasure Island Hotel, inspired by the book of the same name by Robert Louis Stevenson, is a 30-metre pirate ship and a life-size English frigate, multicoloured stand-ins and a 70-minute naval battle which is tirelessly repeated four times a day.

At the Mirage, which cost $650 million in 1990, the attraction consists principally of Siegfried & Roy's white tiger show, the longest non-stop show in Las Vegas (and the one which is always full), but there is an aquarium too, which holds 76,000 litres of salt water, as well as a reconstruction of a rain forest and, most impressive of all, a volcano which erupts every fifteen minutes.

The eruption is complete with flames, steam and smoke issuing from a sort of 16-metre, three-storey, concrete fountain which attracts thousands of people every day.

More modest hotels, especially regarding capacity, include the Hard Rock Hotel with 340 rooms and an "ecological" casino, which aims to attract the younger visitors by devolving part of its takings to save the rain forests and the Debbie Reynolds, which belongs to the Hollywood actress. It has only 197 rooms and has a film museum with over 3000 costumes.

The oriental-style Imperial Palace has an impressive collection of 200 classic cars, from Hitler's Mercedes-Benz to the Alfa Romeo Mussolini gave to Clara Petacci and Al Capone's Cadillac and then there is the equally impressive mega-screen made up of dozens of video screens showing sporting events at the Las Vegas Hilton, which also has an enormous casino and the town's biggest theatre.

114-115 The Las Vegas hotel which has contributed most in transforming the capital of vice into a family entertainment centre is without doubt the Circus&Circus. The hotel, which opened in 1974, was the first to offer rooms at bargain prices, less than $20 dollars, and to give parents the opportunity to have their children looked after while they spent long hours at the gaming tables. Jugglers, trapeze artists, circus performers and, on the mezzanine floor, carnival games for the children are still this entertaining hotel's strong point.

116-117 The Grand Slam Canyon, with its big dippers and Circus&Circus numbers fits perfectly into the strategy which has made Las Vegas one of the principal American tourist centres, beating the celebrated, canonical Mt. Vernon.

118 top Despite the large number of rooms available in the many Las Vegas hotels (seen here, the Monte Carlo, one of the most recent), on average more than 92% of the town's hotel and motel capacity is filled.

118-119 The Hard Rock Café, with its unmistakable giant sign in the shape of an electric guitar, is one of the best-known places in Las Vegas. Las Vegas also has a young people's casino, the Hard Rock Hotel & Casino, which devolves part of its takings towards saving the rain forests.

If the past was glorious and the present is Pharaonic, the future promises to live up to both. The projects pending for millions of cubic metres of new buildings, with investments in the construction sector of $70 million dollars, are, as always, on a grandiose and excessive scale.

Among the newest hotels are: the Bellagio, in Italian style, with 3000 rooms (which costed around $1.1 billion), the New York-New York, (around $460 million), with 2119 rooms, a concentrate of everything the Big Apple has to offer (a 50-metre high replica of the Statue of Liberty and replicas of the Empire State Building, Manhattan and the Brooklyn Bridge) and the Paris Resort Casino, with 2500 rooms, an investment of $420 million with a replica of the Arc de Triomphe, the Champs Elysées, the Seine, the Opéra and the Eiffel Tower. And then the Monte Carlo, inspired by the famous principality, which cost $375 million and has 3024 rooms and the Stratosphere Tower, the highest building (380 metres) west of the Mississippi, with 1500 rooms, three chapels for visitors to get married up in paradise, restaurants and, of course, casinos. For the moment, the plan to build a King Kong which was to have climbed up the tower and swallowed 48 brave (or crazy) passengers down into its stomach has been put on hold.

This is Las Vegas: mad, excessive, pyrotechnic, inimitable, exciting Vegas. Always on the move, always ready to throw itself head-first into the unknown and to bet on itself. For money and for love. A perennial magnet for millions of gamblers from all over the world. And if gambling is part of life's risks, if it is instinctive to the human soul, then you too will not be able to escape its allure. So prepare yourself to throw the dice, while you wait for the next weekend, the one which will make you richer or poorer.

And may luck be with you.

119 The New York-New York, the latest hotel to open on The Strip, at a cost of $460 million, draws its inspiration from the Big Apple during the Twenties and Thirties. Its casino, which has a floor area of 7,432 square metres, houses 2,400 slot machines and 71 gaming tables.

120-121 The number of visitors to the metropolis in the Mojave Desert is continually increasing. A survey carried out by the Las Vegas Convention & Visitors Authority found that in the first six months of 1996 more than 12.2 million tourists chose Las Vegas, an increase of almost 2% over the previous year.

122 The first hotel & casino to open in Las Vegas was the Moulin Rouge, which was inaugurated in 1955. Because of its "historic" value, the Las Vegas City Council is trying everything to prevent it from shutting down

122-123 and 123 top Legends in Concert, a tribute to some of yesterday's superstars, is the famous musical show held every day, except Sunday, in the Imperial Theatre of the Imperial Palace Hotel & Casino. Singers and showmen perform as some

of the most famous people of the period from the Fifties to the Seventies: from Elvis Presley to Judy Garland, Marilyn Monroe and John Lennon. In 1988 the show received the "Show of Shows" award from the International Press Association.

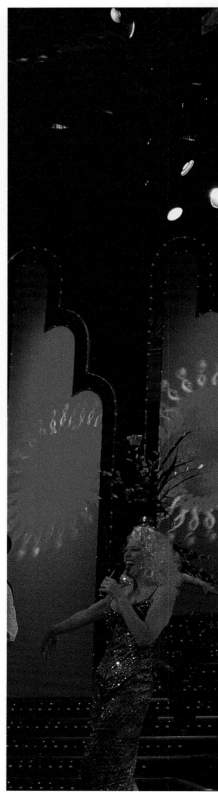

124-125 The sea battle between pirates and the sailors of the English Navy lasts almost seventy minutes, with cannon shots and sword fights between the roughly thirty actors who take part. It is repeated at regular intervals in front of the Treasure Island.

126-127 Las Vegas is continually renewing itself and retains hardly anything of its past. Hotels and other buildings which are only a few decades "old" are razed to make room for other newer and more modern ones, to satisfy the desire for entertainment which characterises the Las Vegas tourist.

128 Neon signs welcome visitors to the Fremont Street Experience, the fantastic light & sound show in Downtown Las Vegas and mark the entrance to the Las Vegas Neon Museum at the west end of the pedestrian precinct.

Las Vegas

LAS VEGAS

ILLUSTRATION CREDITS